AF433956

Commercial Real Estate for Real Estate Agents

Copyright Page

TITLE: Commercial Real Estate for Real Estate Agents

1ST Edition

Copyright @ 2023

Roberto M. Rodriguez. All rights reserved.

ISBN: 9798223436041

Table of Contents

Commercial Real Estate for Real Estate Agents

By Roberto Miguel Rodriguez

Chapter 1: Introduction to Retail Real Estate Mastery

Understanding the Role of Real Estate Agents in the Retail Industry

The retail industry is a dynamic and ever-evolving sector that requires a deep understanding of market trends, consumer behavior, and property management. In this subchapter, we will explore the crucial role that real estate agents play in the retail industry, focusing on their responsibilities, skills, and expertise required to succeed in this niche.

Real estate agents specializing in retail properties, such as shopping centers, malls, and storefronts, serve as the link between property owners and retail businesses. Their primary goal is to facilitate the buying, selling, and leasing of retail spaces, ensuring both parties achieve their objectives.

To effectively navigate the retail real estate market, agents need to possess a comprehensive understanding of the specific needs and challenges faced by retail businesses. This includes knowledge of foot traffic patterns, consumer demographics, and market trends. By staying up-to-date with the latest retail industry news and developments, real estate agents can offer valuable insights and guidance to their clients.

In addition to market knowledge, real estate agents in the retail industry must also possess excellent negotiation skills. They act as intermediaries between property owners and potential tenants, ensuring that lease agreements are fair and beneficial for both parties. Agents must also possess strong communication and interpersonal skills to build relationships with stakeholders and facilitate successful transactions.

Furthermore, real estate agents specializing in retail properties must be well-versed in property management and maintenance. They are responsible for ensuring that retail spaces are well-maintained, clean, and attractive to potential tenants and customers. Additionally, agents must have a keen eye for identifying opportunities for improvement and maximizing the value of retail properties.

Real estate agents in the retail industry can specialize in various niches, including office buildings, industrial real estate, hospitality properties, medical office spaces, mixed-use developments, student housing, self-storage facilities, data centers, and agricultural real estate. Each niche requires a unique set of skills and expertise, and agents must tailor their approach accordingly.

In conclusion, real estate agents play a vital role in the retail industry by bridging the gap between property owners and retail businesses. Their comprehensive market knowledge, negotiation skills, and property management expertise are crucial for successful transactions and the overall growth of the retail sector. Whether specializing in shopping centers, office buildings, or student housing, real estate agents in the retail industry are essential for facilitating the growth and development of retail businesses and properties alike.

Overview of the Retail Real Estate Market

The retail real estate market is a dynamic and ever-changing sector of the real estate industry. It encompasses a wide range of properties, including shopping centers, malls, storefronts, and mixed-use developments. As a real estate agent specializing in retail properties, it is crucial to have a thorough understanding of this market to better serve your clients.

The retail real estate market is influenced by various factors, including consumer behavior, economic conditions, and trends in the retail industry. Understanding these factors can help you make informed decisions when it comes to buying, selling, or leasing retail properties.

One of the key aspects of the retail real estate market is the importance of location. Retail properties need to be strategically located in areas with high foot traffic and good visibility to attract customers. As a real estate agent, your knowledge of the local market and understanding of consumer demographics will play a crucial role in identifying the right location for your clients.

Another important consideration in the retail real estate market is the tenant mix. A successful shopping center or mall relies on a diverse tenant mix that caters to the needs and preferences of the surrounding community. As a real estate agent, you will need to have a thorough understanding of the local market and be able to identify potential tenants that will complement existing businesses and attract a wide customer base.

In recent years, the retail industry has undergone significant changes due to the rise of e-commerce. As a result, traditional brick-and-mortar retailers have had to adapt and innovate to stay competitive. This has led to the emergence of experiential retail and the integration of online and offline shopping experiences. As a real estate agent specializing in retail properties, it is important to stay updated on these trends and understand how they impact the market.

In conclusion, the retail real estate market offers unique opportunities and challenges for real estate agents specializing in this niche. By understanding the factors influencing the market, such as location, tenant mix, and industry trends, you can better serve your clients and help them navigate the complex world of retail real estate.

The Importance of Specializing in Different Property Niches

In the competitive world of real estate, it is essential for agents to differentiate themselves from the crowd. One way to stand out and gain a competitive edge is by specializing in different property niches. By focusing on specific areas of expertise, real estate agents can enhance their knowledge, build a strong network, and provide exceptional service to their clients.

Specializing in different property niches offers numerous benefits for real estate agents. Firstly, it allows agents to develop a deep understanding of the unique dynamics and trends within each niche. For example, specializing in retail properties enables agents to gain insights into the latest consumer behaviors, market demands, and tenant preferences. This knowledge is invaluable when it comes to advising clients on leasing, buying, or selling retail spaces.

Additionally, specializing in different property niches enables agents to build a robust network of industry professionals and potential clients within each niche. By attending industry conferences, joining relevant associations, and actively engaging with peers, agents can establish themselves as experts in their chosen niches. This network not only provides access to exclusive listings and investment opportunities but also establishes credibility and trust among clients.

Moreover, specializing in different property niches allows agents to provide tailored and personalized services to their clients. For instance, an agent specializing in medical office spaces would understand the unique requirements of healthcare professionals, such as compliance with medical regulations and the need for specialized infrastructure. This expertise enables the agent to identify suitable properties that meet the specific needs of their clients, ultimately leading to higher client satisfaction and repeat business.

Lastly, specializing in different property niches opens up new avenues for growth and income diversification. By expanding their knowledge and expertise across various niches, agents can tap into different market segments and capitalize on emerging trends. This diversification not only expands an agent's client base but also provides a buffer against market fluctuations and economic downturns.

In conclusion, specializing in different property niches is of paramount importance for real estate agents. It enhances their knowledge, builds a strong network, enables personalized services, and offers opportunities for growth and income diversification. By becoming experts in niches such as office buildings, retail properties, industrial real estate, hospitality properties, and more, agents can position themselves as trusted advisors and succeed in the competitive real estate industry.

Chapter 2: Office Buildings

Exploring the Office Space Market

In the competitive world of real estate, it is crucial for agents to have a deep understanding of the various niches within the industry. One such niche is the office space market, which caters to businesses in need of professional workspaces. This subchapter will delve into the intricacies of the office space market, providing valuable insights and tips for real estate agents specializing in this area.

Office Buildings: Specializing in buying, selling, and leasing office spaces for businesses.

The office buildings niche is a dynamic and ever-evolving market. As a real estate agent, it is essential to stay updated on the latest trends and demands. Understanding the needs of different businesses and industries will help you identify suitable office spaces that meet their requirements.

Retail Properties: Focusing on shopping centers, malls, and storefronts for retail businesses.

While retail properties primarily cater to the retail industry, they often have office spaces available for lease or purchase. Being knowledgeable about these properties will broaden your expertise and provide added value to your clients.

Industrial Real Estate: Dealing with warehouses, manufacturing plants, and distribution centers.

Although industrial real estate primarily focuses on warehouses and distribution centers, many businesses require office spaces within these facilities. Having a comprehensive understanding of industrial properties will enable you to offer a complete solution to your clients.

Hospitality Properties: Concentrating on hotels, motels, resorts, and other hospitality establishments.

While hospitality properties primarily cater to tourists and travelers, they often have office spaces to support the day-to-day operations of these establishments. Understanding the unique requirements of the hospitality industry will enable you to find suitable office spaces for your clients.

Medical Office Spaces: Catering to healthcare professionals by providing medical office buildings and clinics.

The medical field has specific requirements when it comes to office spaces. Familiarizing yourself with medical regulations, equipment needs, and patient flow will help you identify suitable medical office spaces for healthcare professionals.

Mixed-Use Developments: Specializing in properties that offer a combination of residential, commercial, and retail spaces.

Mixed-use developments, with their diverse range of spaces, often include office spaces. Understanding the dynamics of mixed-use developments will allow you to assist clients looking for a combination of residential and office spaces.

As a real estate agent specializing in office spaces, it is vital to be well-versed in the unique needs and demands of each niche. By exploring the office space market and gaining expertise in various sectors such as retail, hospitality, medical, and industrial, you can offer valuable insights and solutions to your clients. Stay informed, keep learning, and adapt to the ever-changing dynamics of the office space market to become a trusted advisor in this niche.

Buying and Selling Office Spaces

In the competitive world of real estate, understanding the intricacies of buying and selling office spaces is crucial for success. As a real estate agent specializing in office buildings, you play a vital role in connecting businesses with their ideal workspace. This subchapter will provide you with valuable insights and tips to navigate the office real estate market effectively.

When it comes to buying office spaces, it is essential to consider the unique requirements of businesses. Understand their needs in terms of location, size, amenities, and infrastructure. Conduct thorough research on the local market to identify available properties that meet these criteria.

As a real estate agent, you should establish strong relationships with property owners, developers, and landlords. Networking is key in this industry, as it can lead to exclusive access to off-market opportunities that might align perfectly with your clients' needs. Additionally, staying updated with market trends and emerging technology will give you a competitive edge.

When selling office spaces, it's crucial to market the property effectively. Showcase its unique features and advantages, such as proximity to transportation hubs, amenities, and nearby businesses. Utilize both traditional marketing channels and digital platforms to reach a wider audience. Professional photography, virtual tours, and well-crafted property descriptions can significantly enhance your marketing efforts.

Negotiation skills are paramount in the buying and selling process. Help your clients secure the best deal by conducting thorough market analysis, understanding lease terms, and assessing the property's potential for future growth. By demonstrating your expertise and advocating for your clients, you can create win-win situations for all parties involved.

It is also essential to stay updated with local zoning regulations and building codes that may impact the buying and selling process. Being knowledgeable about any potential legal hurdles or environmental considerations will ensure a smooth transaction.

As a real estate agent specializing in office spaces, continuously expanding your knowledge is crucial. Attend industry conferences, seminars, and workshops to stay updated on the latest trends, technologies, and best practices in the market. Building a strong professional network within the commercial real estate community will also provide you with valuable support and potential business opportunities.

Remember, buying and selling office spaces requires a deep understanding of the unique needs and requirements of businesses. By offering exceptional service, leveraging your expertise, and employing effective marketing strategies, you can excel in this niche of the real estate market.

Leasing Strategies for Office Spaces

As a real estate agent specializing in office buildings, it is crucial to have a thorough understanding of leasing strategies for office spaces. The success of your business and the satisfaction of your clients depend on your ability to effectively lease office spaces that meet their unique needs. In this subchapter, we will explore some key strategies that will help you navigate the leasing process and secure the best deals for your clients.

First and foremost, it is essential to thoroughly understand your client's requirements and preferences. Are they looking for a large open plan space or individual offices? Do they require specific amenities or proximity to transportation hubs? By having a detailed understanding of your client's needs, you can narrow down the options and present them with suitable properties.

Next, it is crucial to have a strong network and relationships with property owners and landlords. Building these connections will give you access to the latest listings and off-market opportunities, giving you a competitive edge in finding the perfect office space for your clients. Additionally, having strong relationships with property owners can provide you with valuable insights into their leasing preferences and negotiating strategies.

When negotiating lease terms, it is important to consider factors such as lease duration, rent escalations, and tenant improvement allowances. Understanding market trends and comparable lease agreements in the area will help you negotiate favorable terms for your clients. Additionally, always ensure that the lease agreement is comprehensive and includes clauses that protect your client's interests, such as options to renew or terminate the lease.

To effectively market office spaces, utilize a multifaceted approach. Leverage online platforms, social media, and digital marketing strategies to reach a wide audience of potential tenants. Additionally, consider partnering with local businesses or industry organizations to host networking events and showcase available office spaces.

Lastly, always stay updated on local market trends and changes in regulations that may impact office leasing. Attend industry conferences and seminars, and continuously educate yourself on best practices and emerging technologies in office space leasing.

By employing these leasing strategies, you will be able to effectively cater to your clients in the office building niche and secure successful lease agreements. Your expertise and knowledge will position you as a trusted advisor in the industry, allowing you to build long-term relationships and grow your business.

Chapter 3: Retail Properties

Introduction to Shopping Centers and Malls

Welcome to the subchapter "Introduction to Shopping Centers and Malls" from the book "Retail Real Estate Mastery: Navigating Shopping Centers and Malls." This chapter is specifically addressed to real estate agents specializing in various niches such as office buildings, retail properties, industrial real estate, hospitality properties, medical office spaces, mixed-use developments, student housing, self-storage facilities, data centers, and agricultural real estate.

Shopping centers and malls are integral components of the retail real estate industry. They serve as key destinations for consumers, providing a wide array of retail, dining, entertainment, and service options all under one roof. As a real estate agent, it is crucial to understand the dynamics of these properties to effectively assist your clients in buying, selling, and leasing spaces within them.

In this subchapter, we will explore the fundamental aspects of shopping centers and malls, enabling you to navigate the unique challenges and opportunities they present. We will delve into the various types of shopping centers, ranging from neighborhood centers to regional malls, and discuss their distinctive characteristics, target markets, and tenant mix.

Additionally, we will examine the factors that contribute to the success of shopping centers and malls, such as location, accessibility, parking facilities, anchor tenants, and amenities. Understanding these factors will allow you to identify prime properties and advise your clients on making sound investment decisions.

Moreover, we will explore the evolving trends in the retail industry, including the rise of e-commerce and its impact on brick-and-mortar retail. We will discuss strategies for revitalizing struggling shopping centers and malls, such as incorporating experiential retail concepts, enhancing customer experiences, and embracing omnichannel retailing.

Throughout this subchapter, you will gain valuable insights into the unique considerations and best practices for working with shopping centers and malls. Whether you specialize in retail properties or any other real estate niche, understanding the dynamics of shopping centers and malls will broaden your knowledge and enhance your ability to serve your clients effectively.

So, let's embark on this journey into the world of shopping centers and malls, equipping ourselves with the knowledge and expertise to thrive in the ever-evolving retail real estate market.

Understanding the Retail Business Environment

In the world of real estate, it is crucial for agents to have a comprehensive understanding of the various niches they specialize in. For real estate agents focusing on retail properties, such as shopping centers, malls, and storefronts, it is essential to familiarize themselves with the retail business environment. This subchapter aims to provide a comprehensive overview of the retail business environment, equipping agents with the knowledge they need to excel in this niche.

The retail business environment is a dynamic and ever-changing landscape. Understanding its intricacies is crucial for real estate agents specializing in retail properties. By having a firm grasp of the retail business environment, agents can effectively identify opportunities, negotiate leases, and attract tenants.

One key aspect of understanding the retail business environment is recognizing the factors that influence the success of retail businesses. This includes understanding consumer behavior, market trends, and competition. Agents need to have their finger on the pulse of changing consumer preferences and the latest retail trends in order to position their properties effectively.

Additionally, understanding the unique challenges and considerations that come with retail properties is crucial. This includes knowledge of zoning regulations, lease structures, and tenant mix strategies. Real estate agents must be well-versed in designing lease agreements that align with the needs of retail businesses and ensure a mutually beneficial relationship between landlords and tenants.

Furthermore, real estate agents specializing in retail properties should also be knowledgeable about the latest technologies and innovations shaping the retail industry. From e-commerce and online marketing to smart retail technologies, staying up-to-date with these advancements can help agents better serve their clients and provide valuable insights.

In conclusion, understanding the retail business environment is essential for real estate agents specializing in retail properties. By familiarizing themselves with consumer behavior, market trends, lease structures, and technological advancements, agents can position themselves as experts in this niche. With this knowledge, they can effectively navigate the retail real estate market, attract tenants, and secure successful lease agreements.

Key Considerations for Buying and Selling Retail Properties

As a real estate agent specializing in retail properties, it is crucial to understand the unique dynamics of this market. Whether you are buying or selling shopping centers, malls, or storefronts, there are several key considerations to keep in mind to ensure a successful transaction.

Firstly, location is paramount in retail real estate. The success of a retail property heavily relies on its visibility, accessibility, and proximity to target customers. Before making any decisions, thoroughly research the surrounding area, demographic trends, and potential competition.

Understanding the current and future demand for retail in the location will help you make informed decisions and negotiate better deals.

Another crucial factor to consider is the financial health of the property. Analyze the current and historical financial statements, including income, expenses, and occupancy rates. Look for any potential risks or red flags that may affect the property's value or profitability. It is also essential to evaluate any existing leases, tenant mix, and rental rates to assess the property's income potential.

Additionally, understanding the local zoning and regulatory requirements is vital when dealing with retail properties. Familiarize yourself with the local regulations, permits, and licenses needed for retail businesses in the area. This knowledge will help you guide your clients through the process and avoid any legal complications.

When buying or selling retail properties, it is crucial to consider the current market conditions and trends. Stay updated on the latest retail industry news, consumer preferences, and emerging technologies that may impact the sector. This knowledge will help you position your clients' properties strategically and negotiate better deals.

Lastly, networking is key in the retail real estate industry. Build relationships with potential buyers, sellers, and industry professionals such as developers, brokers, and property managers. Attend industry events, join professional organizations, and leverage online platforms to expand your network and access new opportunities.

In conclusion, buying and selling retail properties requires careful consideration of various factors. By understanding the location, financial health, zoning requirements, market conditions, and networking opportunities, real estate agents specializing in retail properties can navigate the shopping center and mall market successfully. Stay informed, build relationships, and provide valuable insights to your clients to thrive in the retail real estate industry.

Leasing Strategies for Retail Spaces

As a real estate agent specializing in retail properties, it is crucial to have a deep understanding of leasing strategies for retail spaces. With the ever-changing dynamics of the retail industry, it is essential to develop a comprehensive approach that aligns with the needs of both landlords and tenants. This subchapter will explore effective leasing strategies that can help you navigate the world of retail real estate.

1. Understand the Market: Before leasing a retail space, it is essential to conduct thorough market research. This includes analyzing demographics, foot traffic, competition, and consumer behavior in the area. Understanding the market will help you identify the ideal location for your retail clients and negotiate favorable lease terms.

2. Build Strong Relationships: Developing strong relationships with both landlords and tenants is key to successful leasing. For landlords, it is important to showcase your expertise in the retail industry and demonstrate your ability to attract high-quality tenants. For tenants, provide personalized assistance by understanding their business requirements and finding the perfect retail space to meet their needs.

3. Flexible Lease Terms: In the retail industry, flexibility is crucial. Offering flexible lease terms, such as shorter lease durations or options for expansion, can attract a wider range of tenants. This flexibility allows businesses to adapt to market changes and helps landlords maintain a high occupancy rate.

4. Market the Space: Effective marketing is essential to attract potential tenants. Utilize various marketing channels, such as online platforms, social media, and industry-specific publications, to showcase the unique

features of the retail space. Highlight the location's advantages, visibility, foot traffic, and proximity to complementary businesses.

5. Negotiate Favorable Lease Agreements: Negotiating lease agreements is a critical aspect of leasing retail spaces. Work closely with both landlords and tenants to ensure that lease terms are fair and mutually beneficial. Consider factors such as base rent, common area maintenance fees, tenant improvement allowances, and exclusivity clauses.

6. Stay Informed: The retail industry is constantly evolving, and it is crucial to stay informed about market trends, consumer behavior, and emerging technologies. Attend industry conferences, participate in networking events, and engage with industry publications to stay up-to-date with the latest developments in retail real estate.

By implementing these leasing strategies for retail spaces, you can establish yourself as a trusted advisor in the retail real estate market. Your expertise in understanding the unique needs of both landlords and tenants will enable you to secure successful lease agreements and drive long-term profitability for your clients.

Chapter 4: Industrial Real Estate

Overview of Industrial Real Estate

Industrial real estate is a specialized sector within the real estate industry that focuses on the buying, selling, and leasing of warehouses, manufacturing plants, and distribution centers. This subchapter aims to provide real estate agents with a comprehensive understanding of industrial real estate, its unique characteristics, and the opportunities it presents.

Industrial properties are essential for the efficient functioning of businesses involved in production, manufacturing, storage, and distribution. Warehouses, manufacturing plants, and distribution centers are designed to accommodate large-scale operations, with features such as high ceilings, wide open spaces, loading docks, and ample parking. These properties are typically located in industrial parks or areas zoned for industrial use, often situated near transportation hubs, major highways, and logistical infrastructure.

As a real estate agent specializing in industrial properties, you will work closely with businesses looking to lease or purchase suitable spaces for their operations. Understanding the specific needs of industrial clients is crucial, as their requirements may differ significantly from those of other sectors. Factors such as building size, ceiling height, floor load capacity, access to transportation networks, and proximity to suppliers and customers are key considerations in industrial real estate.

Additionally, industrial real estate agents must be well-versed in zoning regulations, environmental considerations, and other legal requirements that may impact industrial operations. This knowledge will enable you to guide clients through the intricacies of acquiring or leasing industrial properties while ensuring compliance with local regulations.

Industrial real estate offers several advantages for investors and businesses alike. The demand for industrial properties remains strong, driven by the growth of e-commerce, globalization, and the need for efficient supply chain management. Furthermore, industrial properties often offer attractive rental yields and long-term lease agreements, providing a stable income stream for investors.

By specializing in industrial real estate, real estate agents can tap into a lucrative niche market and serve the needs of businesses seeking suitable spaces for their operations. Understanding the unique characteristics and demands of industrial properties, as well as staying updated on market trends and investment opportunities, is crucial for success in this sector.

In conclusion, the subchapter "Overview of Industrial Real Estate" provides real estate agents with a comprehensive understanding of the industrial real estate sector. It highlights the unique characteristics of industrial properties, the specific needs of industrial clients, and the opportunities available in this niche market. By specializing in industrial real estate, agents can cater to businesses involved in manufacturing, distribution, and storage, while also capitalizing on the steady demand and attractive returns offered by this sector.

Buying and Selling Warehouses and Distribution Centers

In the world of industrial real estate, warehouses and distribution centers hold a unique and significant role. As a real estate agent specializing in this niche, it is essential to have a thorough understanding of the intricacies involved in buying and selling these properties. This subchapter aims to provide you with the knowledge and expertise required to navigate the complex world of warehouses and distribution centers.

When it comes to buying warehouses and distribution centers, it is crucial to consider several factors. The location of the property is of utmost importance, as accessibility to major transportation routes and logistical hubs can greatly impact its value. Understanding the specific needs of potential buyers, such as the required square footage, ceiling height, and loading capabilities, is essential in identifying the right property to meet their requirements.

In terms of selling warehouses and distribution centers, it is crucial to showcase the property's unique features and advantages. Highlighting factors such as proximity to transportation networks, ample parking and loading areas, and advanced technological infrastructure can significantly impact the selling price. Additionally, understanding the specific needs and preferences of potential buyers, such as e-commerce companies or manufacturing firms, can help tailor the marketing approach and attract the right clientele.

Furthermore, as a real estate agent specializing in industrial properties, it is essential to stay updated on market trends and regulations impacting the warehousing and distribution industry. Understanding the latest advancements in automation and technology can provide valuable insights when advising clients on potential investments. Moreover, staying informed about zoning regulations, environmental considerations, and local market dynamics is crucial in ensuring a smooth transaction process.

Lastly, building strong relationships with key players in the warehousing and distribution industry, such as logistics companies, manufacturers, and supply chain managers, can provide a competitive edge. These relationships can lead to valuable referrals and insider knowledge, enabling you to better serve your clients and provide them with the best possible options.

In conclusion, buying and selling warehouses and distribution centers requires specialized knowledge and expertise within the niche of industrial real estate. By understanding the unique requirements of potential buyers, staying updated on market trends, and fostering relationships within the industry, real estate agents can successfully navigate this complex market and provide exceptional service to their clients.

Leasing Strategies for Industrial Properties

As a real estate agent specializing in industrial real estate, it is crucial to understand the unique leasing strategies that can help you effectively market and lease industrial properties such as warehouses, manufacturing plants, and distribution centers. This subchapter will provide you with key insights and practical tips to navigate the industrial leasing market successfully.

1. Identify Target Tenants: Start by identifying the target tenants for industrial properties. These may include logistics and distribution companies, manufacturers, wholesalers, and e-commerce businesses. Understanding their specific requirements and preferences will help you tailor your leasing strategy accordingly.

2. Highlight Key Features: Emphasize the key features of the industrial property, such as its location, accessibility to major transportation routes, proximity to ports or airports, and availability of amenities like loading docks, ample parking space, and high ceilings. These features are critical for businesses in the industrial sector.

3. Network with Local Businesses: Build strong relationships with local businesses in the industrial sector. Attend industry events, join relevant associations, and participate in networking activities to expand your network. These connections can help you identify potential tenants and generate leads.

4. Offer Flexible Lease Terms: Industrial tenants often require flexibility in terms of lease duration. Consider offering flexible lease terms, such

as short-term leases, lease extensions, or lease-to-own options, to accommodate their specific needs.

5. Understand Zoning and Regulations: Familiarize yourself with the zoning regulations and permits required for industrial properties in your area. Ensure that the property meets all necessary requirements and can be used for the intended industrial purposes.

6. Conduct Comprehensive Due Diligence: Before listing an industrial property, conduct thorough due diligence. Assess the property's condition, including its structural integrity, mechanical systems, and compliance with safety regulations. Provide potential tenants with accurate and detailed information to build trust and streamline the leasing process.

7. Market Effectively: Develop a comprehensive marketing strategy to attract potential tenants. Utilize online platforms, industry-specific publications, and targeted advertising campaigns to reach the industrial sector. Highlight the property's unique selling points and showcase its potential for businesses.

8. Offer Competitive Pricing: Research the local market to determine competitive rental rates for industrial properties. Offer competitive pricing based on market trends, the property's condition, and the amenities it offers. Consider incentives such as rent abatement or tenant improvement allowances to attract tenants.

By implementing these leasing strategies, you can position yourself as an expert in industrial real estate and successfully lease industrial properties to businesses in need. Stay updated on market trends, maintain strong relationships with potential tenants, and adapt your strategies to meet the evolving needs of the industrial sector.

Chapter 5: Hospitality Properties

Introduction to the Hospitality Industry

In the fast-paced world of real estate, it is crucial for agents to have a comprehensive understanding of various niches within the industry. One such niche that holds immense potential for growth and profitability is the hospitality industry. This subchapter aims to provide real estate agents with a solid introduction to the hospitality industry, equipping them with the necessary knowledge and insights to navigate this particular market segment effectively.

Hospitality properties, such as hotels, motels, resorts, and other establishments, present unique opportunities and challenges for real estate agents. Understanding the dynamics of this industry is essential for professionals specializing in buying, selling, and leasing hospitality properties.

The hospitality industry is a vital component of the overall real estate market, catering to the needs of business and leisure travelers alike. As the world becomes increasingly interconnected and travel becomes more accessible, the demand for hospitality properties continues to grow.

Real estate agents focusing on hospitality properties must be well-versed in the specific requirements and considerations associated with this niche. They need to understand the factors that contribute to the success of hospitality establishments, such as location, amenities, customer service, and market trends.

Moreover, agents specializing in hospitality properties should be familiar with the various types of establishments within this sector. From boutique hotels to large resorts, each category presents unique investment opportunities and requires tailored marketing and management strategies.

Additionally, understanding the financial aspects of the hospitality industry is crucial for real estate agents. This includes analyzing revenue streams, occupancy rates, and operating expenses to determine the potential profitability of a hospitality property.

Furthermore, agents must be knowledgeable about industry regulations and compliance requirements specific to hospitality properties. This includes understanding zoning laws, permits, licensing, and safety regulations, among other considerations.

By gaining a comprehensive understanding of the hospitality industry, real estate agents specializing in hospitality properties can effectively serve their clients and capitalize on the immense potential this sector offers. Whether it is assisting with the acquisition of a hotel property or helping a client lease a resort space, agents with expertise in the hospitality industry are well-positioned to thrive in this competitive market.

In conclusion, the hospitality industry presents a unique and lucrative opportunity for real estate agents. By familiarizing themselves with the intricacies of this niche, agents specializing in hospitality properties can provide valuable services to their clients and achieve success in this dynamic and ever-growing sector of the real estate market.

Buying and Selling Hotels, Motels, and Resorts

Buying and selling hotels, motels, and resorts can be a lucrative endeavor for real estate agents specializing in hospitality properties. This subchapter will provide valuable insights and strategies for agents looking to navigate this unique sector of the market.

When it comes to buying hotels, motels, and resorts, thorough due diligence is essential. Agents must consider factors such as location, market demand, competition, and potential for growth. Conducting a comprehensive market analysis and feasibility study will help agents identify viable investment opportunities and determine a property's value.

In terms of selling hospitality properties, agents must be adept at marketing and positioning the asset to attract potential buyers. This may involve creating compelling listing materials, leveraging online platforms, and networking within the industry. It is crucial for agents to highlight the property's unique selling points, such as its amenities, reputation, and potential for revenue generation.

Understanding the financial aspects of hotel, motel, and resort transactions is also crucial. Agents must be well-versed in evaluating a property's revenue streams, including room rates, occupancy rates, and ancillary services such as food and beverage or event spaces. Additionally, knowledge of financing options specific to the hospitality industry, such as Small Business Administration (SBA) loans or hotel-specific lenders, can greatly assist both buyers and sellers.

Navigating the legal and regulatory landscape is another important aspect of dealing with hospitality properties. Agents must be familiar with zoning regulations, permits, licenses, and compliance requirements specific to hotels, motels, and resorts. Engaging with legal professionals who specialize in hospitality real estate can help ensure a smooth and compliant transaction process.

Furthermore, agents should consider forming strategic partnerships with professionals in related fields, such as hotel management companies, architects, and interior designers. These collaborations can provide valuable expertise and resources to clients and enhance the overall value proposition of the property.

In conclusion, buying and selling hotels, motels, and resorts requires specialized knowledge and expertise. Real estate agents in the hospitality sector must conduct thorough due diligence, understand the financial aspects of the industry, navigate legal and regulatory requirements, and leverage strategic partnerships to maximize value for their clients. With the right approach, this niche can offer lucrative opportunities and a rewarding career for real estate professionals specializing in hospitality properties.

Leasing Strategies for Hospitality Establishments

Introduction:

In the ever-evolving world of commercial real estate, the hospitality sector has gained significant attention in recent years. As real estate agents specializing in commercial properties, it is crucial to understand the unique leasing strategies that can help maximize the potential of hospitality establishments. Whether it's hotels, restaurants, or entertainment venues, this subchapter will delve into the key considerations and effective leasing tactics that cater to the needs of both property owners and tenants.

Understanding the Hospitality Market:

Before diving into leasing strategies, it is essential to comprehend the dynamics of the hospitality market. Real estate agents need to stay updated on the latest industry trends, local market demands, and target audience preferences. By having a deep understanding of the market, agents can better advise their clients on leasing opportunities, property types, and potential risks.

Strategic Location Selection:

Choosing the right location is vital for any hospitality establishment's success. Real estate agents should assist their clients in identifying areas with high foot traffic, proximity to transportation hubs, and sufficient parking facilities. Additionally, understanding the target demographic and local competition can help in selecting the ideal location for a hospitality property.

Negotiating Favorable Lease Terms:

When it comes to leasing hospitality establishments, negotiating favorable lease terms is crucial. Real estate agents should guide their clients through the lease negotiation process, ensuring that both parties benefit from the agreement. This includes negotiating reasonable rental rates, lease duration, renewal options, and maintenance responsibilities. Agents should also consider the potential for revenue sharing arrangements based on the property's performance, which can be advantageous for both landlords and tenants.

Adapting to Changing Consumer Preferences:

Hospitality establishments must continuously adapt to changing consumer preferences. Real estate agents can play a pivotal role in advising property owners on the importance of flexible lease terms that allow for modifications and renovations to meet evolving market demands. This may include reconfiguring spaces, incorporating technological advancements, or diversifying the property's offerings.

Building Strong Tenant-Landlord Relationships:

Successful leasing strategies for hospitality establishments require building strong relationships between tenants and landlords. Real estate agents should emphasize the importance of effective communication, understanding, and collaboration between the two parties. By fostering positive relationships, agents can help ensure long-term lease agreements, tenant satisfaction, and increased property value.

Conclusion:

Leasing hospitality establishments within the commercial real estate sector requires a comprehensive understanding of the industry's unique dynamics. Real estate agents must grasp the evolving market trends, strategic location selection, effective lease negotiation, adaptability, and building strong tenant-landlord relationships. By employing these leasing strategies, agents can assist their clients in maximizing the potential of their hospitality properties and navigating the ever-changing landscape of the commercial real estate market.

Chapter 6: Medical Office Spaces

Understanding the Healthcare Market

In the world of real estate, it is crucial for professionals to have a comprehensive understanding of different markets and industries. One such market that offers tremendous opportunities is the healthcare sector. This subchapter aims to provide real estate agents with an in-depth understanding of the healthcare market, specifically focusing on medical office spaces and clinics.

The healthcare market is a unique and specialized sector that requires specific knowledge and expertise. As a real estate agent specializing in medical office spaces, it is essential to grasp the nuances of this market to effectively serve healthcare professionals and their unique needs.

First and foremost, understanding the healthcare market requires knowledge of the healthcare industry itself. Real estate agents should familiarize themselves with the latest trends and developments in healthcare, including advancements in medical technology, changes in healthcare policies, and the evolving needs of healthcare professionals.

Additionally, it is essential to understand the specific requirements of medical office spaces and clinics. Healthcare professionals have unique needs when it comes to their workspace. They require facilities that can accommodate medical equipment, provide ample parking for patients, and offer a convenient location for both healthcare providers and their patients.

Real estate agents specializing in medical office spaces should also be aware of the regulatory and compliance requirements that apply to healthcare facilities. This includes understanding zoning regulations, building codes, and other legal considerations specific to the healthcare industry.

Furthermore, building relationships with healthcare professionals and key stakeholders in the healthcare industry is crucial for success in this market. This can include networking with physicians, medical groups, and hospital administrators. By establishing strong relationships, real estate agents can gain valuable insights and referrals within the healthcare market.

Finally, staying updated on the latest market trends and opportunities is essential. The healthcare market is dynamic and constantly evolving, with new medical facilities and clinics being established regularly. Real estate agents must stay ahead of the curve by monitoring market trends, attending industry conferences, and leveraging technology to identify potential opportunities.

In conclusion, understanding the healthcare market is vital for real estate agents specializing in medical office spaces and clinics. By familiarizing themselves with the healthcare industry, understanding the specific requirements of healthcare professionals, and building relationships within the healthcare community, real estate agents can position themselves as trusted advisors in this lucrative market.

Buying and Selling Medical Office Buildings and Clinics

As a real estate agent specializing in medical office spaces, you play a crucial role in connecting healthcare professionals with the right properties to establish their practices. Buying and selling medical office buildings and clinics requires a unique understanding of the needs and requirements of healthcare professionals, as well as the ever-evolving healthcare industry.

When it comes to buying medical office buildings and clinics, there are several factors to consider. Location is key, as healthcare professionals often prefer properties that are easily accessible to patients and have ample parking space. Proximity to hospitals, pharmacies, and other medical facilities is also important.

In addition to location, you should also pay attention to the layout and design of the property. Medical office spaces need to be functional and adaptable to the specific needs of different specialties. For example, a dental clinic may require specific plumbing and electrical requirements, while a pediatrician's office may need child-friendly waiting areas.

When selling medical office buildings and clinics, it is essential to highlight the unique features and benefits of the property. Emphasize any existing medical infrastructure, such as examination rooms, surgical suites, or radiology facilities. Highlight the potential for expansion or customization to attract healthcare professionals looking to grow their practices.

It is also important to stay up-to-date with the latest trends and changes in the healthcare industry. For instance, the rise of telemedicine has increased the demand for medical office spaces that are equipped with the necessary technology and infrastructure to support virtual consultations. Understanding these trends can give you a competitive edge and help you match healthcare professionals with properties that meet their specific needs.

Lastly, building strong relationships within the healthcare community is crucial for success in this niche. Attend medical conferences and events, network with healthcare professionals, and collaborate with medical associations to establish yourself as a trusted advisor in the field. By doing so, you can become the go-to real estate agent for buying and selling medical office buildings and clinics.

In conclusion, buying and selling medical office buildings and clinics require a deep understanding of the healthcare industry, as well as the specific needs of healthcare professionals. By focusing on location, design, highlighting unique features, staying informed about industry trends, and building strong relationships within the healthcare community, you can excel in this specialized niche of real estate.

Leasing Strategies for Medical Office Spaces

As a real estate agent specializing in medical office spaces, it is crucial to have a comprehensive understanding of the unique leasing strategies that apply to this niche. Medical office spaces cater to healthcare professionals and require specific considerations to ensure the success of the leasing process. This subchapter will provide you with valuable insights and strategies to navigate the leasing of medical office spaces effectively.

1. Understand the needs of healthcare professionals: Medical office spaces need to accommodate the specialized requirements of healthcare professionals. This may include specific infrastructure, equipment, and compliance with healthcare regulations. Familiarize yourself with these needs and ensure that the properties you offer meet them.

2. Location is key: Healthcare professionals often prefer convenient locations with easy accessibility for their patients. Consider factors such as proximity to hospitals, transportation links, and parking facilities when selecting medical office spaces to lease. Highlight these benefits to potential tenants.

3. Build relationships with healthcare organizations: Develop strong connections with local hospitals, clinics, and healthcare networks. These organizations often have leasing needs or can refer healthcare professionals seeking office spaces. Networking and building relationships will increase your chances of securing quality tenants.

4. Offer flexible lease terms: Healthcare professionals may require flexibility in lease terms due to changing medical needs or the possibility of expanding their practice. Consider offering options such as shorter lease periods or the ability to upgrade to larger spaces within the same

building. This flexibility can attract tenants and lead to longer-term relationships.

5. Provide value-added services: Differentiate yourself from competitors by offering value-added services. This could include assistance with zoning and building permits, connections to medical equipment suppliers, or referrals to healthcare-specific interior designers. By going the extra mile, you can position yourself as a trusted advisor and attract more clients.

6. Maintain a professional network: Collaborate with other professionals in the medical industry, such as medical equipment suppliers, architects, and healthcare consultants. By having a network of trusted contacts, you can provide additional resources and support to healthcare professionals during the leasing process.

7. Stay updated on healthcare regulations: Medical office spaces need to comply with specific healthcare regulations, such as the Health Insurance Portability and Accountability Act (HIPAA). Stay informed about these regulations and ensure that the properties you offer meet the necessary standards. This knowledge will instill confidence in potential tenants.

By implementing these leasing strategies, you can position yourself as a trusted partner for healthcare professionals in search of medical office spaces. Understanding their unique needs, providing value-added services, and developing strong relationships within the medical community will set you apart from competitors and lead to successful lease agreements.

Chapter 7: Mixed-Use Developments

Exploring Mixed-Use Properties

In the ever-evolving world of real estate, mixed-use properties have emerged as a highly sought-after investment opportunity. Combining residential, commercial, and retail spaces within a single development, these properties offer a unique value proposition for both investors and tenants alike. This subchapter will delve into the intricacies of exploring mixed-use properties, providing real estate agents with valuable insights to navigate this growing market segment.

For real estate agents specializing in various niches such as office buildings, retail properties, industrial real estate, hospitality properties, medical office spaces, student housing, self-storage facilities, data centers, and agricultural real estate, understanding the nuances of mixed-use developments can open up new avenues for success.

Mixed-use properties present a diverse range of benefits. They create vibrant communities that cater to the needs of residents, employees, and shoppers all in one location. This integration fosters a sense of convenience, as individuals can live, work, shop, and play within the same vicinity. As a real estate agent, being able to identify and highlight these advantages is crucial in attracting potential buyers or tenants.

To effectively explore mixed-use properties, agents must familiarize themselves with the zoning regulations, planning processes, and market trends specific to this type of development. Understanding the intricacies of zoning laws and planning regulations governing mixed-use properties is essential in guiding clients through the complexities of acquiring, developing, or leasing such properties.

Additionally, agents should stay informed about the latest market trends, such as the growing demand for mixed-use properties in urban areas or the integration of sustainability features in these developments. This knowledge will enable agents to provide valuable insights to their clients and position themselves as trusted advisors in the industry.

Furthermore, networking and building relationships with key stakeholders in the mixed-use development sphere, including architects, developers, and lenders, can prove invaluable. These connections can provide agents with access to off-market opportunities and help them stay ahead of the competition.

In conclusion, exploring mixed-use properties offers real estate agents specializing in various niches a unique opportunity to diversify their portfolios and tap into a growing market segment. By understanding the intricacies of this type of development, staying informed about market trends, and building relationships with industry professionals, agents can position themselves as experts in the field and unlock new pathways to success.

Buying and Selling Properties with Residential, Commercial, and Retail Spaces

As a real estate agent specializing in various niches, it is crucial to have a comprehensive understanding of buying and selling properties with residential, commercial, and retail spaces. This subchapter will delve into the intricacies of these transactions and provide you with essential knowledge to navigate the dynamic world of retail real estate.

Residential properties play a significant role in the real estate market. Understanding the needs and preferences of homebuyers is essential for successful transactions. From single-family homes to multi-unit residential buildings, knowing the market trends, pricing strategies, and effective marketing techniques is crucial to attract potential buyers and negotiate favorable terms.

Commercial properties, such as office buildings, require a unique approach. Specializing in this niche involves catering to businesses looking for suitable workspace. As a real estate agent, you need to understand the specific requirements of businesses, including location, amenities, and infrastructure. Building relationships with landlords, property owners, and business owners is vital to sourcing and closing lucrative deals.

Retail properties, including shopping centers, malls, and storefronts, present their own set of challenges and opportunities. Understanding consumer behavior, foot traffic patterns, and tenant mix is crucial. By staying up-to-date with the latest retail trends, you can assist retail businesses in finding the perfect location to maximize their visibility and profitability.

Industrial real estate, which encompasses warehouses, manufacturing plants, and distribution centers, requires a specialized skill set. Knowledge of zoning regulations, logistics, and transportation infrastructure is vital in assisting clients in this niche. Understanding the needs of industrial tenants, such as storage space, loading docks, and proximity to transportation hubs, will enable you to identify suitable properties and negotiate favorable terms.

Hospitality properties, including hotels, motels, resorts, and other establishments, require a unique approach. Understanding the tourism industry, market demand, and guest preferences is essential. By providing expertise in property selection, pricing strategies, and marketing techniques, you can assist clients in maximizing their return on investment in the hospitality sector.

Medical office spaces cater to healthcare professionals seeking specialized facilities. Understanding the unique requirements of medical practitioners, such as proximity to hospitals, accessibility, and specialized infrastructure, is crucial. By specializing in medical office buildings and clinics, you can provide tailored solutions to healthcare professionals looking for suitable spaces.

Mixed-use developments offer a combination of residential, commercial, and retail spaces. Understanding the dynamics of these properties, including zoning regulations, tenant mix, and community planning, is essential. By specializing in mixed-use developments, you can help clients find properties that offer a diverse range of income streams and attract a wide customer base.

In conclusion, as a real estate agent specializing in various niches, it is vital to have a deep understanding of buying and selling properties with residential, commercial, and retail spaces. By equipping yourself with knowledge of market trends, consumer behavior, and industry-specific requirements, you can provide valuable expertise to clients in the office buildings, retail properties, industrial real estate, hospitality properties, medical office spaces, mixed-use developments, student housing, self-storage facilities, data centers, and agricultural real estate niches.

Leasing Strategies for Mixed-Use Developments

Mixed-use developments have become increasingly popular in the world of real estate, offering a unique combination of residential, commercial, and retail spaces. As a real estate agent specializing in mixed-use developments, it is crucial to understand the leasing strategies that can maximize the potential of these properties. In this subchapter, we will explore some key strategies to help you navigate the leasing process in mixed-use developments.

1. Understanding the Target Demographic: Each mixed-use development caters to a specific target demographic. It is essential to identify the ideal tenants for each component of the development. For example, residential spaces may be more appealing to young professionals or families, while retail spaces may attract local businesses or national

brands. By understanding the target demographic, you can tailor your leasing efforts accordingly.

2. Synergy and Compatibility: One of the main advantages of mixed-use developments is the synergy created between different components. Ensure that the businesses and tenants within the development complement each other. For instance, a residential building may benefit from having a convenience store or a coffee shop nearby. By curating a mix of tenants that work well together, you can create a thriving community within the mixed-use development.

3. Flexibility in Leasing Terms: Mixed-use developments often require flexibility in leasing terms to accommodate a variety of businesses. Offer different lease options, such as short-term leases for pop-up shops or longer-term leases for established businesses. Flexibility in leasing terms can attract a wider range of tenants and maximize occupancy rates.

4. Promote Convenience and Accessibility: Emphasize the convenience and accessibility of mixed-use developments to potential tenants. Highlight the benefits of having residential, commercial, and retail spaces in one location, such as reduced commuting time and increased foot traffic for businesses. Additionally, ensure that the development has ample parking, public transportation access, and other amenities that enhance convenience for tenants and customers.

5. Effective Marketing and Networking: Leasing in mixed-use developments requires effective marketing and networking strategies. Utilize online platforms, social media, and traditional marketing channels to reach potential tenants. Attend industry events, networking sessions, and engage with local businesses to build relationships and attract suitable tenants.

In conclusion, leasing strategies for mixed-use developments require a deep understanding of the target demographic, synergy between tenants, flexibility in leasing terms, promotion of convenience and accessibility, and effective marketing and networking. By implementing these strategies, real estate agents specializing in mixed-use developments can maximize occupancy rates and create thriving communities within these unique properties.

Chapter 8: Student Housing

Introduction to the Student Housing Market

The student housing market is a unique and thriving niche within the real estate industry. With the increasing number of students pursuing higher education and the demand for convenient and affordable accommodations near colleges and universities, this market presents a lucrative opportunity for real estate agents specializing in student housing.

In this subchapter, we will explore the dynamics of the student housing market and the key factors that real estate agents should consider when dealing with properties in this niche. We will delve into the specific needs and preferences of student tenants, the rental market trends, and the various strategies that can be employed to maximize returns in this segment.

One of the primary advantages of investing in student housing is the consistent demand. Students require a place to live while pursuing their education, and many prefer to live off-campus in properties that offer proximity to their college or university. This demand ensures a steady stream of potential tenants, reducing the risk of vacancies and providing a reliable income source for property owners.

Understanding the unique needs of student tenants is crucial for real estate agents in this market. Students generally seek affordable accommodations with convenient access to campus, amenities, and transportation. They often prefer shared living spaces to reduce costs and foster a sense of community. Additionally, safety and security are paramount considerations for both students and their parents.

To successfully navigate the student housing market, real estate agents should stay informed about the local rental market trends and regulatory requirements. They should have a deep understanding of the rental rates, occupancy rates, and the supply-demand dynamics in the area. This knowledge will allow them to accurately advise their clients on pricing, property management, and investment opportunities.

Furthermore, real estate agents specializing in student housing should be well-versed in marketing strategies tailored to attract student tenants. Utilizing online platforms, social media, and partnerships with educational institutions can help agents effectively reach their target audience and promote their properties.

Overall, the student housing market offers a promising opportunity for real estate agents looking to expand their expertise and cater to the needs of this specific niche. By understanding the unique dynamics, preferences, and trends of the student housing market, agents can position themselves as trusted advisors and provide valuable guidance and services to both property owners and student tenants.

Buying and Selling Properties for Student Accommodation

In recent years, student housing has emerged as a lucrative niche market for real estate agents. As more students pursue higher education, the demand for suitable accommodation near colleges and universities has skyrocketed. This subchapter explores the ins and outs of buying and selling properties for student accommodation, providing valuable insights and strategies for real estate agents specializing in this niche.

When it comes to buying properties for student accommodation, location is key. Proximity to educational institutions, amenities, and public transportation are crucial factors that attract students. Real estate agents should identify areas with high student populations and potential for growth. Researching local housing trends and understanding the needs and preferences of students will help agents make informed decisions.

Additionally, real estate agents must consider the specific requirements of student accommodation properties. Shared living spaces, communal facilities, and security features are essential for student housing. Agents should be knowledgeable about local regulations and zoning laws pertaining to student accommodation to ensure compliance and avoid legal issues.

Selling student accommodation properties requires a targeted marketing strategy. Real estate agents should leverage digital platforms, social media, and partnerships with educational institutions to reach their target audience. Highlighting the property's proximity to campus, amenities, and safety features will attract student tenants and their parents.

Furthermore, real estate agents specializing in student accommodation should stay updated on market trends and rental rates. Understanding the rental market and demand-supply dynamics will help agents determine the optimal pricing strategy for their clients. Providing accurate financial projections and potential rental income to potential buyers will enhance the value proposition of the property.

To excel in this niche, real estate agents should also develop strong relationships with key stakeholders in the student accommodation industry. Building partnerships with property management companies, student unions, and educational institutions can provide agents with valuable leads and referrals.

In conclusion, buying and selling properties for student accommodation offers real estate agents a unique opportunity to cater to the growing demand for housing near colleges and universities. By understanding the specific requirements of student tenants, staying updated on market trends, and developing strategic partnerships, real estate agents can thrive in this niche market and provide valuable solutions to both buyers and sellers in the student housing sector.

Leasing Strategies for Student Housing

As a real estate agent specializing in various niches, it is essential to have a comprehensive understanding of leasing strategies for different property types. When it comes to student housing, there are specific considerations and approaches that can maximize your success in this market.

1. Location is Key: When dealing with student housing, proximity to colleges and universities is crucial. Students prefer properties that are within walking distance or have easy access to campus. Understanding the local transportation options and amenities such as grocery stores, restaurants, and recreational facilities can help you identify the most attractive locations for student housing.

2. Collaborate with Educational Institutions: Building relationships with colleges and universities can be highly beneficial. By partnering with these institutions, you can gain insight into their housing needs, upcoming projects, and even be recommended as a trusted real estate agent. This collaboration can give you a competitive edge and help you stay informed about the changing demands of the student housing market.

3. Understand Student Preferences: To effectively lease student housing, it is essential to understand their preferences. Many students seek affordable options with shared living spaces, communal areas, and amenities such as study rooms, fitness centers, and laundry facilities. Offering flexible lease terms and furnished options can also attract more students to your properties.

4. Utilize Digital Marketing: In today's digital age, it is essential to have a strong online presence to attract student tenants. Utilize social media platforms, targeted advertising, and online listing platforms to showcase your student housing properties. Highlight the key features and benefits

that appeal to students, such as a safe environment, proximity to campus, and a vibrant student community.

5. Offer Competitive Pricing and Incentives: The student housing market can be highly competitive. To stand out from the crowd, consider offering competitive rental rates and attractive incentives. This could include discounted rent, free parking, or even partnerships with local businesses to provide exclusive student discounts.

6. Build Relationships with Student Organizations: Engaging with student organizations can help you reach a larger audience of potential tenants. Collaborate with student associations, clubs, and organizations to sponsor events, offer scholarships, or provide resources specifically tailored to student housing. This involvement can create a positive reputation and word-of-mouth referrals.

7. Stay Up-to-Date with Regulations: Student housing regulations can vary from city to city, so it is crucial to stay informed about local laws and regulations. Ensure that your properties comply with safety codes, proper licensing, and any other requirements specific to student housing.

By implementing these leasing strategies, real estate agents specializing in student housing can position themselves as experts in this niche market. Understanding the unique needs of students and adapting your approach accordingly will help you attract and retain tenants in this lucrative sector.

Chapter 9: Self-Storage Facilities

Understanding the Self-Storage Market

As a real estate agent, it is crucial to have a comprehensive understanding of various niches in the industry. One such niche is the self-storage market, which deals with the buying, selling, and managing of storage units and facilities. This subchapter aims to provide real estate agents with valuable insights into the self-storage market and its potential for investment and growth.

The self-storage market has experienced significant growth in recent years, driven by various factors. One key factor is the increasing trend of downsizing and decluttering, as people seek to simplify their lives and make better use of their living spaces. This has created a high demand for self-storage units, both for personal and business use.

When it comes to self-storage facilities, location is crucial. Real estate agents specializing in self-storage facilities should focus on identifying areas with a high population density, limited storage options, and a growing demand for storage space. Urban areas, college towns, and rapidly developing suburbs are often excellent locations for self-storage facilities.

In addition to location, real estate agents should also consider the size and amenities of the self-storage units. Offering a range of unit sizes to accommodate different storage needs is essential. Additionally, amenities such as climate control, 24/7 access, and security features can attract more customers and increase the value of the facility.

Understanding the target market is another essential aspect of the self-storage market. Real estate agents should be familiar with the demographics and preferences of potential customers. This knowledge can help in marketing the facility effectively and tailoring the offerings to meet the specific needs of the target market.

Moreover, it is crucial to stay updated with the latest trends and technologies in the self-storage industry. The rise of mobile apps, online booking systems, and smart security solutions has revolutionized the way self-storage facilities operate. Real estate agents should be knowledgeable about these advancements and guide their clients in adopting them to stay competitive in the market.

In conclusion, the self-storage market presents a lucrative opportunity for real estate agents looking to diversify their portfolio. Understanding the factors driving the market's growth, identifying favorable locations, and catering to the specific needs of the target market are key to success in this niche. By staying updated with industry trends and technologies, real estate agents can position themselves as experts in the self-storage market and provide valuable guidance to their clients.

Buying and Selling Storage Units and Facilities

As a real estate agent specializing in various niches such as office buildings, retail properties, industrial real estate, and more, it is essential to understand the unique dynamics of buying and selling storage units and facilities. This subchapter will provide you with valuable insights into the self-storage industry and equip you with the knowledge necessary to navigate this market successfully.

The self-storage industry has experienced significant growth in recent years, making it an attractive investment opportunity. As a real estate agent, you may encounter clients interested in purchasing or selling storage units or facilities. Understanding the key factors that influence the value and profitability of these properties will allow you to provide accurate and informed advice to your clients.

When it comes to buying self-storage units, location is a critical factor. Areas with high population density, limited storage options, and strong demand for storage space are ideal for investment. Conducting thorough market research and analyzing demographic data will help you identify areas with the potential for high occupancy rates and rental income.

In terms of selling storage units, emphasizing the property's unique selling points is crucial. Highlighting features such as climate control, security systems, and convenient access will attract potential buyers. Additionally, providing detailed financial information, including occupancy rates, rental income, and expenses, will instill confidence in potential buyers and help justify the asking price.

It is also essential to understand the operational aspects of managing storage units and facilities. Familiarize yourself with industry best practices, including tenant screening procedures, rental agreements, and maintenance protocols. This knowledge will enable you to guide your clients in making informed decisions and ensure the smooth operation of their self-storage investments.

Lastly, staying informed about industry trends and developments is vital in the fast-paced world of self-storage. Keep an eye on technological advancements, such as smart security systems and online rental platforms, which can enhance the value and efficiency of storage facilities.

In conclusion, buying and selling storage units and facilities can be a lucrative venture for real estate agents specializing in various niches. By understanding the unique dynamics of the self-storage industry, conducting thorough market research, and staying informed about industry trends, you can provide exceptional service to your clients and capitalize on this growing market.

Managing Self-Storage Properties

In the realm of real estate, self-storage facilities have emerged as a lucrative niche, offering a unique investment opportunity for discerning real estate agents. This subchapter will delve into the intricacies of managing self-storage properties, providing valuable insights and strategies tailored to the needs of real estate professionals specializing in various niches, including office buildings, retail properties, industrial real estate, hospitality properties, medical office spaces, mixed-use developments, student housing, data centers, and agricultural real estate.

Self-storage facilities are a dynamic asset class that requires a distinct approach to management. Understanding the key elements of effective self-storage property management is essential for maximizing returns and ensuring long-term success. From acquiring suitable properties and optimizing occupancy rates to implementing robust security measures and fostering positive tenant relationships, this subchapter will cover all aspects of managing self-storage properties.

To begin, we will explore the process of acquiring self-storage properties, including evaluating market demand, conducting due diligence, and negotiating favorable deals. Real estate agents specializing in different niches will gain valuable insights into the unique factors to consider when acquiring self-storage facilities, such as location, competition, and potential for expansion.

Next, we will delve into strategies to optimize occupancy rates and maximize revenue streams. This will include effective marketing techniques to attract and retain tenants, implementing dynamic pricing strategies, and offering value-added services. Real estate agents specializing in retail properties, mixed-use developments, and student housing will find specific strategies tailored to their niches, taking into account the unique requirements of their target demographic.

Additionally, we will address the importance of implementing robust security measures to safeguard tenants' belongings and ensure peace of mind. This subchapter will provide guidance on selecting state-of-the-art security systems, training staff on security protocols, and maintaining a safe and secure environment.

Lastly, we will emphasize the significance of fostering positive tenant relationships to enhance customer satisfaction and encourage long-term tenancies. From providing exceptional customer service to addressing concerns promptly, real estate agents will learn strategies to cultivate a loyal tenant base in the competitive self-storage market.

By delving into the nuances of managing self-storage properties, this subchapter equips real estate agents with the knowledge and tools to navigate this unique niche successfully. Whether specializing in office buildings, industrial real estate, or agricultural properties, real estate professionals will gain valuable insights to capitalize on the tremendous potential offered by self-storage facilities.

Chapter 10: Data Centers

Overview of Data Center Properties

In today's digital age, data centers play a crucial role in supporting the technology infrastructure of businesses across various industries. As a real estate agent specializing in data centers, it is important to have a comprehensive understanding of these unique properties. This subchapter will provide you with an overview of data center properties, their features, and the key considerations when buying, selling, or leasing them.

Data centers are purpose-built facilities designed to house computer systems, servers, and networking equipment. They serve as the backbone for storing, processing, and distributing vast amounts of data. These properties require specific infrastructure and amenities to ensure the reliable operation of mission-critical systems.

When dealing with data center properties, it is important to consider factors such as location, power supply, cooling systems, security measures, connectivity options, and scalability. The location of a data center is crucial, with factors such as proximity to fiber optic networks, access to reliable power grids, and favorable natural disaster risk profiles being key considerations.

Power supply is critical for data centers, as they require a continuous and reliable source of electricity. Data centers often have redundant power systems, including backup generators, to ensure uninterrupted operation. Cooling systems are also essential to maintain optimal temperature and humidity levels within the facility, as heat generated by the equipment can be significant.

Security is of utmost importance in data centers due to the sensitive nature of the data they house. These properties often have multiple layers of physical and digital security measures, including surveillance systems, biometric access controls, and fire suppression systems.

Connectivity options are crucial for data centers, as they need high-speed and reliable internet connectivity. Data centers are typically located near major network hubs to ensure low-latency connections and robust connectivity options for clients.

Scalability is another key factor in data center properties. As businesses grow, their data storage and processing needs increase. Data centers should have the flexibility to accommodate future expansion and upgrades without disrupting ongoing operations.

As a real estate agent specializing in data centers, it is essential to have a deep understanding of these properties' technical requirements, industry standards, and emerging trends. By staying informed and knowledgeable, you can provide valuable insights and guidance to clients looking to buy, sell, or lease data center properties.

In the next chapters, we will delve deeper into the specifics of data center design, market trends, financial considerations, and the unique challenges and opportunities that come with this niche in the real estate industry.

Buying and Selling Data Centers

In the rapidly evolving digital age, data centers have become an integral part of our society. As a real estate agent specializing in data centers, you have a unique opportunity to serve a niche market that is in high demand. This subchapter will provide you with essential knowledge and strategies for buying and selling data centers, ensuring that you can navigate this specialized field with confidence.

Data centers are specialized properties designed to house computer systems and store vast amounts of data. With the exponential growth of online activities, businesses and organizations increasingly rely on data centers to support their operations. As a real estate agent, understanding the unique requirements and challenges associated with data centers will enable you to provide valuable services to your clients.

When buying or selling a data center, it is crucial to consider factors such as location, infrastructure, security, and connectivity. Data centers are typically situated in areas with reliable power sources, robust internet connectivity, and proximity to major cities. Assessing the facility's power capacity, cooling systems, and redundancy measures is essential to ensure it can meet the demands of its users.

Security is another critical aspect of data centers. Clients entrust their valuable data to these facilities, so implementing robust security measures is paramount. Familiarize yourself with industry-standard security protocols, including biometric access control, surveillance systems, and fire suppression systems. Understanding these security features will help you assess the value and level of protection offered by a data center.

Additionally, it is essential to stay informed about the latest technological advancements and industry trends. The data center landscape is constantly evolving, with innovations such as edge computing and cloud services reshaping the market. Keeping up-to-date with these advancements will enable you to provide valuable insights to your clients and position yourself as a trusted advisor in the field.

In conclusion, buying and selling data centers requires a specialized understanding of the unique requirements and challenges associated with these properties. By familiarizing yourself with the factors mentioned above and staying informed about industry trends, you can provide exceptional service to your clients in this niche market. Data centers are vital components of our digital infrastructure, and as a real estate agent specializing in this field, you play a pivotal role in facilitating their growth and success.

Key Considerations for Data Center Management

As a real estate agent specializing in various niches, including data centers, it is important to understand the key considerations for effective data center management. Data centers play a vital role in our increasingly connected world, housing crucial computer systems and data storage for businesses. Here are some important factors to consider when managing data centers:

1. Location: The location of a data center is crucial. It should be situated in an area with reliable power supply, access to high-speed internet connectivity, and minimal risk of natural disasters such as floods or earthquakes. Proximity to major cities and transportation routes is also important for ease of access.

2. Security: Data centers hold sensitive and valuable information, making security a top priority. Implementing robust security measures such as surveillance systems, access controls, and fire suppression systems is essential. Regular security audits and monitoring should be conducted to ensure the safety of the facility.

3. Redundancy and Backup Systems: To minimize downtime and ensure continuous operation, data centers require redundant power and cooling systems. Backup generators, uninterruptible power supply (UPS) units, and redundant network connections are essential to handle unexpected power outages or equipment failures.

4. Scalability and Flexibility: Data centers need to be designed with scalability in mind. As businesses grow, their data storage requirements increase. The facility should have the ability to accommodate future expansion and upgrades. Additionally, the infrastructure should be

flexible enough to adapt to changing technology trends and industry standards.

5. Energy Efficiency: Data centers consume a significant amount of energy, so incorporating energy-efficient practices is crucial. This includes using energy-efficient cooling systems, optimizing server layouts for better airflow, and implementing virtualization technologies to maximize resource utilization.

6. Compliance and Regulations: Data centers often handle sensitive data and must comply with various regulations, such as data protection laws, industry-specific standards, and privacy regulations. It is important to stay up-to-date with the latest compliance requirements and ensure the data center meets all necessary certifications.

7. Maintenance and Monitoring: Regular maintenance and monitoring are essential for optimal data center performance. This includes conducting routine equipment checks, monitoring temperature and humidity levels, and performing preventive maintenance to identify and address potential issues before they become critical.

By considering these key factors, real estate agents specializing in data centers can provide their clients with valuable insights and guidance. Effective data center management is crucial for businesses relying on these facilities to ensure the security, reliability, and scalability of their critical data and systems.

Chapter 11: Agricultural Real Estate

Introduction to Agricultural Properties

As a real estate agent specializing in various niches such as office buildings, retail properties, industrial real estate, hospitality properties, medical office spaces, mixed-use developments, student housing, self-storage facilities, data centers, and agricultural real estate, it is crucial to have a comprehensive understanding of each niche. In this subchapter, we will delve into the world of agricultural properties and explore the unique aspects and considerations associated with this niche.

Agricultural real estate deals with properties related to farming, ranching, and agricultural operations. These properties can range from small family farms to large-scale commercial farms, and they play a vital role in the production and distribution of food and other agricultural products.

One of the key factors to consider when dealing with agricultural properties is the location. Factors such as soil quality, climate, water availability, and proximity to markets and transportation infrastructure significantly impact the suitability and value of agricultural land. Understanding these factors and their impact on the property's potential is essential for effectively assisting clients in the agricultural sector.

Additionally, it is crucial to be familiar with the various types of agricultural properties. These can include crop farms, livestock farms, orchards, vineyards, and aquaculture operations, among others. Each type of property requires specific knowledge and expertise to evaluate its potential and marketability accurately.

Furthermore, understanding the unique challenges and regulations associated with agricultural properties is essential. These can include zoning restrictions, environmental regulations, water rights, and tax considerations. Familiarity with these aspects will enable you to provide valuable guidance to clients and navigate potential obstacles effectively.

In the agricultural real estate niche, it is also important to stay informed about industry trends and emerging technologies. Advancements in precision agriculture, sustainable farming practices, and alternative energy sources are transforming the agricultural sector. Keeping up with these developments will allow you to provide innovative solutions to clients and position yourself as a knowledgeable and trusted advisor.

In conclusion, agricultural properties offer unique opportunities and challenges for real estate agents. Understanding the specific considerations associated with these properties, including location, property types, regulations, and industry trends, is crucial for success in this niche. By gaining expertise in agricultural real estate, you can effectively assist clients involved in farming, ranching, and other agricultural operations and contribute to the growth and sustainability of the agricultural sector.

Buying and Selling Farming and Ranching Land

Buying and selling farming and ranching land is a unique niche within the real estate industry, catering to individuals and organizations involved in agricultural operations. As a real estate agent specializing in agricultural real estate, it is crucial to understand the specific dynamics and considerations involved in this sector.

When it comes to buying agricultural land, it is essential to consider factors such as soil quality, water availability, and proximity to markets. Farmers and ranchers rely on fertile soil for successful cultivation, so understanding the different soil types and their suitability for specific crops or livestock is crucial. Additionally, assessing the water sources and irrigation systems available on the property is vital for efficient farming practices.

Proximity to markets and transportation infrastructure is another critical factor to consider. Farmers and ranchers need convenient access to distribution channels and potential buyers for their produce or livestock. Understanding the local market demand and analyzing transportation options, such as nearby highways or railroad access, can greatly impact the property's value.

Selling agricultural land requires a comprehensive understanding of the potential buyer's needs and expectations. Marketing the property to farmers, ranchers, or agricultural investors can be different from traditional real estate marketing strategies. Highlighting the property's agricultural potential, existing infrastructure, and any additional features, such as barns or equipment storage, can attract potential buyers.

As a real estate agent specializing in agricultural real estate, it is essential to stay updated on industry trends, government regulations, and incentives related to farming and ranching. Familiarizing yourself with local agricultural organizations and attending industry events can help you build a network and stay informed about market opportunities.

Navigating the buying and selling process for farming and ranching land requires a unique set of skills and knowledge. By understanding the specific needs of farmers, ranchers, and agricultural investors, you can provide valuable insights and guidance throughout the transaction process. With the right expertise and a deep understanding of the agricultural real estate market, you can become a trusted advisor for your clients in this specialized niche.

Leasing Strategies for Agricultural Operations

As a real estate agent specializing in agricultural real estate, it is important to understand the unique leasing strategies and considerations for agricultural operations. Whether you are working with farmers, ranchers, or other agricultural businesses, having a solid understanding of their needs and goals will greatly enhance your ability to provide valuable services.

One key aspect to consider when leasing agricultural properties is the length of the lease. Unlike other commercial real estate sectors, agricultural leases often span longer timeframes. Farmers and ranchers typically require leases of several years or even decades to ensure stability and continuity in their operations. As a real estate agent, it is important to negotiate lease terms that meet the specific needs of your agricultural clients while also protecting the interests of the property owner.

Another crucial factor to consider is the type of agricultural operation being conducted on the property. Different types of farming, ranching, and agricultural businesses have distinct requirements and may require specialized infrastructure. For example, a dairy farm will require barns, milking parlors, and storage facilities, while a vineyard will need irrigation systems and wine production facilities. Understanding these unique needs will help you identify suitable properties and negotiate lease terms that align with the specific requirements of the agricultural operation.

Additionally, it is important to consider the potential for diversification in agricultural properties. Many farmers and ranchers are looking to diversify their businesses to include agritourism, farm-to-table operations, or even renewable energy projects. By understanding these emerging trends and opportunities, you can help your agricultural clients identify properties with the potential for additional income streams and assist them in navigating the complexities of lease agreements for these diversified operations.

Lastly, staying up-to-date with local and regional agricultural regulations is crucial. Understanding zoning laws, water rights, and environmental regulations will enable you to guide your clients through the leasing process and ensure compliance with all legal requirements.

In conclusion, leasing agricultural properties requires a specialized understanding of the unique needs and considerations of farmers, ranchers, and other agricultural businesses. By considering lease length, specific operational requirements, potential for diversification, and local regulations, you can provide valuable services to your agricultural clients and help them find the perfect property to support their operations.

Chapter 12: Conclusion and Future Trends in Retail Real Estate Mastery

Recap of Key Concepts

In this subchapter, we will recap the key concepts covered in "Retail Real Estate Mastery: Navigating Shopping Centers and Malls." As real estate agents specializing in various niches such as office buildings, retail properties, industrial real estate, hospitality properties, medical office spaces, mixed-use developments, student housing, self-storage facilities, data centers, and agricultural real estate, it is crucial to have a solid understanding of the fundamental principles and strategies that govern the retail real estate market.

First and foremost, we emphasized the importance of location. As real estate agents, you understand that location is a critical factor in determining the success of any property. When it comes to retail properties, the location is even more crucial. Retail businesses rely heavily on foot traffic, visibility, and accessibility. Therefore, it is essential to assess the demographics, population density, and local market dynamics when evaluating potential retail spaces.

Furthermore, we delved into the various types of retail properties, including shopping centers, malls, and storefronts. Each has its unique characteristics and considerations. Shopping centers are typically anchored by one or more major retailers and offer a mix of retail, dining, and entertainment options. Malls, on the other hand, are larger-scale shopping complexes with a wider range of amenities. Storefronts, often found in urban areas, cater to small retailers and provide a street-level presence.

We also explored the specific needs and requirements of other niches, such as office buildings, industrial real estate, hospitality properties, medical office spaces, mixed-use developments, student housing, self-storage facilities, data centers, and agricultural real estate. Each of these niches has its distinct set of considerations, including zoning regulations, building requirements, and market trends.

Throughout the book, we emphasized the importance of staying up-to-date with industry trends, market data, and technology. As real estate agents, it is crucial to continuously educate ourselves and adapt to the evolving needs of our clients. By leveraging technology, market research, and networking opportunities, you can position yourself as a trusted advisor to clients in the retail real estate market.

In conclusion, this subchapter offered a comprehensive recap of key concepts essential for real estate agents specializing in various niches within the retail real estate market. By understanding the fundamentals of location, property types, and niche-specific considerations, you will be well-equipped to navigate the intricacies of retail real estate and provide valuable guidance to your clients.

Emerging Trends in the Retail Real Estate Market

As a real estate agent specializing in retail properties, it is crucial to stay up-to-date with the emerging trends in the retail real estate market. Understanding these trends can provide you with a competitive edge and enable you to better serve your clients. In this subchapter, we will explore some of the key emerging trends that are shaping the retail real estate market today.

1. E-commerce Impact: With the rise of e-commerce, traditional brick-and-mortar retailers are facing new challenges. However, this has also created opportunities for retail real estate agents. Businesses are seeking to establish a physical presence to complement their online operations, leading to the emergence of experiential retail and pop-up

stores. As an agent, you can help retailers find unique spaces that enhance their brand experience.

2. Mixed-Use Developments: The demand for mixed-use developments is on the rise. These developments offer a combination of residential, commercial, and retail spaces, creating vibrant communities. Real estate agents with expertise in mixed-use developments can capitalize on this trend by connecting retail businesses with these integrated spaces.

3. Sustainability and Green Buildings: In recent years, there has been a growing emphasis on sustainability and green buildings. Retailers are increasingly conscious of their environmental impact and are seeking properties that align with their sustainability goals. Agents who understand green building practices and can identify eco-friendly properties will have an advantage in attracting environmentally conscious retailers.

4. Technology Integration: Technology is transforming the retail experience, and real estate agents need to adapt accordingly. Retailers are incorporating technologies such as augmented reality, virtual reality, and AI-powered chatbots into their physical stores. Agents who are knowledgeable about these technologies can assist retailers in finding spaces that accommodate their tech-driven strategies.

5. Localization and Community Engagement: Retailers are recognizing the importance of connecting with local communities. They are seeking locations that allow them to engage with customers on a more personal level. As an agent, you can help retailers identify properties in neighborhoods that align with their brand values and target demographics.

By staying informed about these emerging trends, real estate agents specializing in retail properties can position themselves as valuable resources for their clients. Whether it's assisting with the integration of technology, finding unique spaces for experiential retail, or identifying sustainable properties, being ahead of the curve will enable you to provide exceptional service and help your clients thrive in the ever-evolving retail real estate market.

Tips for Success as a Real Estate Agent in Retail Properties

As a real estate agent specializing in retail properties, there are several key strategies and tips that can help you achieve success in this niche. Whether you are focused on shopping centers, malls, or storefronts for retail businesses, these tips will help you navigate the unique challenges and opportunities in the retail real estate market.

1. Build a strong network: Networking is crucial in the real estate industry, and it is especially important when working with retail properties. Connect with local business owners, property managers, and developers to establish relationships and gain insights into the market. Attend industry events and join professional organizations to expand your network further.

2. Stay updated on market trends: Retail is a dynamic industry, and it is essential to stay informed about the latest market trends, consumer behaviors, and technological advancements. Subscribe to industry publications, attend conferences, and participate in training programs to enhance your knowledge and expertise.

3. Understand the tenant's perspective: To effectively serve your retail clients, it is crucial to understand their needs and expectations. Put yourself in their shoes and consider factors such as foot traffic, visibility, accessibility, and local competition when evaluating potential properties. This will help you identify the most suitable locations for your clients.

4. Develop marketing expertise: Marketing plays a vital role in retail real estate. Master the art of showcasing retail properties by utilizing high-quality visuals, virtual tours, and compelling property descriptions.

Leverage digital marketing platforms and social media to reach a wider audience and attract potential tenants.

5. Collaborate with professionals: Retail properties often require collaboration with other professionals such as architects, contractors, and interior designers. Build relationships with these experts to ensure seamless transactions and provide valuable resources to your clients.

6. Stay ahead of regulations: Retail properties are subject to various regulations and zoning laws. Stay updated on local regulations, permits, and licensing requirements to guide your clients through the process smoothly. Partner with legal professionals familiar with retail real estate to ensure compliance.

7. Embrace technology: Technology has revolutionized the real estate industry, and as a retail property specialist, it is essential to leverage these advancements. Utilize property management software, online listing platforms, and virtual tools to streamline processes and enhance client experiences.

Remember, success in retail real estate requires dedication, market knowledge, and a customer-centric approach. By following these tips, you can position yourself as a trusted advisor to retail clients and achieve long-term success in this rewarding niche.

www.ingramcontent.com/pod-product-compliance
Lightning Source LLC
Chambersburg PA
CBHW021755150726
47989CB00004B/1673